RESENTMENT TO RECONNECTION

A MAN'S GUIDE TO OVERCOMING PERSONAL AND MARITAL CONFLICT

SVEN MASTERSON

COPYRIGHT

For permission requests, write to the publisher at:

Sven Masterson, LLC
320 Gold Ave. SW Ste. 620
Albuquerque, NM 87102 USA

Second Edition

Library of Congress Cataloging-in-Publication Data

Names: Sven Masterson, author.

Title: Resentment To Reconnection / Sven Masterson

Description: Second Edition. | Albuquerque: Sven Masterson, LLC, 2024. | Includes bibliographical references and index.

Identifiers:

- (ebooks) ISBN 979-8-89443-305-9 | ISBN 978-1-304-37435-6
- (paperbacks) ISBN 9798325201196 | ISBN 9798224571055 | ISBN 978-1-304-36532-3

Subjects: LCSH: Marriage—psychological aspects. | Interpersonal relations. | Self-help. | BISAC: FAMILY & RELATIONSHIPS / Marriage & Long-Term Relationships. | SELF-HELP / Personal Growth / Happiness.

Classification: LCC HQXXXX .M37 2024 | DDC 306.8—dc23

Cover design by Sven Masterson

First Printing, 2024

CONTENTS

FOREWORD

I always like to review the Forward section in the books I read.

I'm curious about who influenced the author and who their mentors were. I want to know what their relationship with the author was like...were they just professional acquaintances or truly good friends? I never cared for people who introduced others as My good friend! when you know, they are not really friends at all.

I also want the Forward section to reassure me that I'm in the right place and that this book will be enjoyable.

I have now been asked to write one of those sections. So, I will tell you what I would want to know if I were in your shoes right now.

Sven Masterson and I have been ACTUAL friends and colleagues for nearly seven years at this writing.

We've had endless phone calls, Zoom calls, and personal, face-to-face conversations over dinner, drinks, and fires. We've covered topics I can only discuss with deep thinking, deep feeling, and deeply trusting people. We share a common set of values around the profession of Men's Coaching and how we can best serve men in the most positive, mature, and emotionally healthy ways.

Yes, he was a client of mine in the early days. Since then, I've witnessed him launch his thinking, his voice, and his passion for serving men into the world. The Masterful Men community he created is a treasure trove of free resources and higher-level personal growth opportunities.

Every word, every idea, every pain, and every insight Sven shares in this book is directly from his own experience of life, love, and marriage.

His views and lessons about self-reliance, dependency, ownership, and brotherhood come from a life lived out loud. His wisdom is guided by hard-earned lessons—both wild failures and amazing successes.

Sven does not regurgitate the quotes and memes you'll find on social media. His expression and language are 100% authentic and curated from the same pain, struggle, doubt, uncertainty, and fears that may have brought you to this book. He clearly demonstrates why vulnerability is a super-power. And he will make you feel safe in taking your first steps to realizing your own superpower.

In Chapter 10, he shares a story about his father and a lawn tractor incident that led him to a self-destructive conclusion that he could not ask for help and that he was his only reliable resource. In his words, This belief followed me into adulthood and into my marriage, where it initially manifested as a refusal to seek support and ask others for help or to share my vulnerabilities genuinely.

Sven masterfully explains the paradox of achieving a high level of self-reliance while becoming more powerfully open-hearted, emotionally connected, and spiritually generous in all of your relationships.

He shares such specific and heart-breaking details about his life with his wife, Zelda, that you'll wonder if he's afraid she will read this book! (I know she has, and she's totally cool with it!)

I recommend you read the entire book because there are golden nuggets everywhere.

Sven's mission is clearly to serve men and the women who try to love us. Make sure you get to Chapter 20 where he answers the most common "Yeah, buts..." we face in our client work all the time. For example, you must read his answers to questions like this:

Yeah, but if we are supposed to be emotionally self-reliant and self-source our emotional needs, what is the point of relationships?

And...

Yeah, but what if my partner doesn't notice or appreciate my efforts to change?

Enjoy the book and enjoy your journey. As you'll find in the book, it's a waste of time trying to figure this out on your own. It takes courage to ask for help. Hell, it took courage for you to read this Forward section!

As Sven says at the end of the book, *Here's to a lifetime of learning, growth, and profound transformation!*

Warm wishes,
Steve Horsmon
Founder of GoodGuys2GreatMen
https://www.goodguys2greatmen.com

INTRODUCTION

THE BREAKING POINT – A JOURNEY FROM DESPAIR TO DISCOVERY

Welcome to my journey—a path that spiraled from silent suffering to a place of profound understanding and connection. My name is Sven Masterson, and I want to share with you not just a story of personal transformation but an invitation to a life-changing realization that can reshape how you view yourself and your relationships.

EARLY DAYS: A PROMISE MADE

My relationship with Zelda began with promise and passion. We married young, full of dreams and aspirations. I envisioned a life filled with love and partnership, where we would support and uplift each other. Instead, as years passed, our interactions became transactions—each of us keeping score, slowly building resentment.

THE HIDDEN AGONY

From the outside, our life together looked successful. We had a beautiful home on a sprawling 25-acre property and six wonderful children whom Zelda schooled at home while I ran a thriving consulting business as a software architect. I was respected in our community and seen as a leader. Yet, internally, I was crumbling. I harbored a dark secret that I could barely admit to myself—I sometimes wished Zelda would die in her sleep so I could re-marry and start over with someone else. This thought wasn't born out of anger or malice; it stemmed from profound dissatisfaction, despair, and desperation, a yearning to escape from the pain that eventually became a constant companion.

THE DESCENT INTO RESENTMENT

My role as the sole breadwinner while Zelda homeschooled our children became a source of silent contention. My efforts, risks, and sacrifices seemed to go unnoticed and unappreciated. I felt invisible in my home, unrecognized by the person whose opinion mattered most. Despite external successes, I felt like a failure in my partner's eyes and, even worse, my own.

As the years wore on, this internal battle deepened. My attempts to be the hero, the knight in shining armor for Zelda, were met with what felt like indifference and sometimes hostility. She seemed perpetually closed off—an emotional distance that left me perpetually asking, "Is everything okay?" Her reserved nature, which I had once hoped to 'rescue' her from, now felt like a chasm between us.

Things worsened, and my constant inner mantra became, "Is this all there is?" and "Am I only here to wait out my days in utilitarian service to others?" I lived in a Groundhog Day existence where life became monotonous, feeling like all I was good for was earning money, providing security, giving rides, and fixing broken things. I felt like a cash machine, Uber driver, security guard, handyman, and rarely much more. I was tired of feeling like I didn't matter, alone in a crowd, unseen, unappreciated, and unloved.

A STRUGGLE WITH TEMPTATION

As my marital dissatisfaction deepened, so did a dangerous temptation—a lure that threatened to unravel the fabric of my commitments. My struggles were compounded by an emotional void that Zelda, encased in her reserved demeanor, seemed unable to fill. My heart ached for a connection, a validation of my masculinity and efforts, which I felt were perpetually dismissed or undervalued at home. This void became a breeding ground for fantasies of escape, which revolved around other women who seemed to recognize and admire the qualities in me that Zelda overlooked.

THE LONGING FOR APPRECIATION

It began innocuously—a smile from a woman at a conference, a compliment from a friend's wife, each interaction tinged with a recognition I desperately craved. These women were not just acknowledging my professional successes; they seemed to appreciate me at a fundamental level. They laughed at my jokes, valued my opinions, and looked at me in ways that made me feel seen and understood—feelings I had not experienced in a long time.

This appreciation, or the lack thereof at home, starkly contrasted my life. Every interaction with another kind, soft, available woman illuminated the growing darkness of my marriage. These interactions increasingly captivated me, each adding fuel to a dangerous fire within me.

THE EMOTIONAL DILEMMA

The more I felt ignored and unappreciated by Zelda, the more I noticed and was drawn to these other women. This wasn't a mere physical attraction or raw lust—it was an emotional and psychological yearning for validation. Each seemingly innocent conversation with another woman who offered warmth and understanding became a salve for my wounded ego but also a step closer to betrayal—betrayal of my vows and of the woman I had once loved so deeply, and betrayal of the personal relationships our family had with some of these women.

As these feelings grew, so did my frustration, guilt, and shame. I knew the dangerous path I was treading, yet the fantasy of a fresh start with someone who saw the best in me was intoxicating and consumed my thoughts. It was a mental escape from the reality of a marriage that felt more like a prison with each passing day.

THE JUSTIFICATION OF DAYDREAMS

These daydreams were my secret escape. They offered me a glimpse of a life where I was appreciated and adored. I began to justify these fantasies as harmless. After all, I wasn't acting on them; I was imagining a different life. But deep down, I knew these thoughts were eroding my commitment to Zelda and our marriage. They were signs of profound unhappiness that I was too scared to confront directly.

WHY NOT JUST GET A DIVORCE?

You might be wondering why I didn't just file for divorce and move on. Fair question! I'd been raised in an environment where marriage was forever and "til death do us part." I'd also wanted to be a husband and father since my earliest memories and the thought of the pain and anguish I believed my children would experience if I divorced was just too much to bear. But also, even though I didn't know it at the time, I was suffering the same ailment that all men in such places are suffering from - waiting for people and circumstances outside of me to change. But they didn't change, not for the better, at least. But they did get worse.

CONFRONTING THE REALITY

My first turning point came when I realized that these fantasies were not just escapes but symptoms of deeper issues in my marriage and within myself. They were wake-up calls, urging me to confront the dissatisfaction and disconnect I felt at home. It was a painful acknowledgment that if I didn't take action, these daydreams could quickly morph into realities that would devastate everyone involved.

This realization was both sobering and clarifying. It propelled me towards seeking help, which was no small task. Everywhere I looked for guidance, I found platitudes, judgments, and a lot of "Job's Comforters." "Where are all the older, wiser men?" I pondered angrily. "Where were all the goddamned mentors?!" I found myself increasingly saying in the privacy of my loneliness.

Eventually, I was able to reconnect with an older, wiser family friend — "Uncle Ed", from my past who could guide me through the extreme parts of the crisis. He was a true saint, spending countless hours with me at Panera Bread in my hometown. He patiently listened to my complaints, grievances, pain, and frustration —all without judgment. He'd been there, and it was evident in the wisdom he shared with me. It was beneficial, and I experienced relief from some acute pain. Yet, it was also three hours from my home and infrequent. Nevertheless, it was enough to stop the bleeding, and I'd soon be on a slow path to restorations.

Unfortunately, I did what many men often do - I got comfortable and complacent.

IT'S ALWAYS THE LITTLEST THINGS

With six kids and a wife beside me every night, I'd experienced countless no or low-sleep nights given to crying babies, sick children, bad dreams, and every other thing that ruins a husband and father's sleep. Through it all, I'd never left our room to find a quieter place to sleep, and I prided myself on such dedication. So, upon getting a nasty respiratory infection resulting in a terrible cough, I became shocked and incredulous when Zelda spent several nights in the guest room so I would not disturb her sleep. This reconnected me with my old friend, resentment, and I began to slide back into my pain once again.

During this time, I also learned that Zelda had confided in a friend some of her struggles due to me sorting through my relationship and emotions toward a female friend of ours. Zelda's friend didn't keep that confidence but then went on to share with others that I was an adulterer and philanderer. As a man who'd always lived a life of trying to do the right thing and who was working so hard to overcome temptation, I was furious and exasperated, wishing I'd just cheated on my relationship since I was effectively living in a world of consequences as though I had done so. What was the point? I constantly asked myself.

FINDING COMMUNITY AND CONNECTION WITH MEN

At that time, through a series of random events, I stumbled upon a video thumbnail of a men's coach named Steve Horsmon that piqued my curiosity. I watched it and thought, "This guy makes a lot of sense. It's like he's under my couch!" Steve ended his video by offering a free consultation call with anyone who contacted him. So, I set up a call with Steve to vent and get some perspective.

But that's not what happened. Instead of encouraging me that my anger and resentment were justified, Steve provided a different perspective that challenged my current mindset. He encouraged me to reconsider my approach to my marital problems and personal frustrations. He showed me how to move away from resentment and contempt by showing me how to see Zelda with empathy and compassion. Then, he invited me into a community of other men to join him for a week-long retreat to Mexico, which I'd go on to do months later.

That day, a profound shift began, creating an avalanche of transformation in my life. Finding Steve and a men's community ultimately led me to experience the transformative principles of Unconditional High Regard, Ownership, Self-Reliance, and Brotherhood. These principles didn't just help me salvage my marriage; they guided me in redefining my sense of self-worth and reshaping my interactions with Zelda and others.

The journey from temptation to transformation was fraught with challenges but was necessary. It led me to a deeper understanding of my needs and desires and, more importantly, how to fulfill them in healthy and affirming ways, not just for me but for my marriage. This section of my story, laden with vulnerability and struggle, sets the stage for the profound changes that followed, changes that I am eager to share in the hopes that they may guide you on your path to fulfillment and connection.

This book is my heartfelt invitation to you—whether you're struggling in silence or simply seeking a deeper connection. Join me as we explore these transformative principles together. Let's embark on this journey to repair what is broken and discover a new way of living that brings true fulfillment and joy.

In the following chapters, I'll walk you through these transformative keys. I'll share the exact moments of despair, the insights that struck me, what I've discovered about resentment, dependency, and insecurity, and how applying these principles step by step led to a marriage and a life filled with love and laughter—without starting over with a new lover.

If you've ever felt stuck, misunderstood, or on the brink of giving up on your relationship, this book is for you. Join me on this transformation journey, and let's unlock the door to a more fulfilling life together.

PART ONE
DEPENDENCY, INSECURITY, AND RESENTMENT

Not everything that is faced can be changed, but nothing can be changed until it is faced.
— James Baldwin

ONE
UNDERSTANDING RESENTMENT

Resentment is the poison you swallow hoping the other person will die.

　— Unknown

~

R esentment is a subtle yet profound force that can erode the foundations of relationships. Unlike anger, which is loud and immediate, resentment builds slowly, coloring perceptions and interactions with a persistent shade of discontent. This chapter explores the roots and manifestations of resentment and provides pathways to overcoming it through emotional self-reliance and understanding.

THE ROOTS OF RESENTMENT

Resentment often begins when there is a perceived imbalance —an unchecked emotional ledger where the give-and-take becomes unfavorably skewed. It grows in the soils of unmet expectations, where the seeds of dependency are sown. We experience resentment when we believe that others owe us more than they provide, whether it is respect, appreciation, or love.

THE PENNY METAPHOR

The dynamics of an emotional economy can be understood through the metaphor of pennies, which I have used to help many men grasp the complexities of their emotional inter-actions:

Imagine being brought into a room with nine other people. Each of you is given thirty pennies, but you are told you cannot live a fully satisfying life unless you collect one hundred pennies. However, no additional pennies will be introduced into this closed system. It quickly becomes apparent that not everyone can reach the goal without taking pennies from someone else. These feelings of scarcity create an environment ripe for conflict and resentment. Some might hoard their pennies, others might beg or steal, and some might band together to pool their resources at the expense of others.

People grow desperate, asking one another for pennies. Yet, each person is experiencing the same dilemma. For anyone to exit the room, some must have pennies, and some must not. There are innate winners and losers.

This scenario is a powerful allegory for how we often handle our emotional needs. We enter relationships with a deficit mindset, believing we need others to 'top us up.' When they fail to do so, or when the emotional exchange feels uneven, resentment takes root.

I like this metaphor because it raises some key attributes of the worldview in which most men I encounter are living.

PENNILESS WORLDVIEW ATTRIBUTES:

Artificial Scarcity

We grow up learning that our pennies come to us through achievement, performance, acceptance, approval, and validation of others. This inevitably places us in a scarcity mindset, where people and circumstances don't consistently provide us with enough pennies to meet the "100 pennies" requirement for a satisfactory life. This scarcity creates a foundation for the emotional deficiencies we often feel.

Competition and Conflict

The scarcity we accept necessitates that individuals either take from others or form alliances to pool resources, leading to competition and potential conflict. This mirrors how people sometimes handle their emotional needs, competing for emotional resources such as acceptance, approval, validation, value, worth, respect, and love from others. This creates a transactional, commercial "love" in relationships that eventually leads to emotional and relational bankruptcy.

Dependence and Resentment

When we believe that not everyone can achieve 100 pennies without taking from others, we naturally depend on others for emotional fulfillment. This dependence creates insecurity because we fear that others won't reliably give us our pennies, withholding them and placing us in danger. We believe others should provide us with pennies and keep us secure. When they don't, we begin to experience resentment when the needs are unmet or when the emotional exchanges feel unfair.

Zero-Sum Game

This worldview is a zero-sum game where one person's gain is another's loss. It reflects relationships in which individuals feel that for them to feel happy or fulfilled, someone else must provide for or sacrifice their emotional needs.

Systemic Flaws and Personal Disempowerment

The system inherently creates "winners" and "losers," indicating that it's flawed. This leads to societal or relational systems that disempower individuals, making them unable to meet their needs independently.

IS THERE A BETTER WAY?

Yes, there is! I've witnessed many men, including myself, leave the penniless worldview behind, with it, their resentment, contempt, hostility, stonewalling, disconnection, and broken, crumbling relationships. They've done this by experiencing two fundamental shifts in their understanding of the world.

First, they possess **inherent wholeness** and begin to believe that individuals are inherently born whole with all the 'pennies' they need. They slowly realize that they have internal resources and do not need to depend on others to feel complete, thus advocating for self-reliance and inner fulfillment.

They then experience a second, fundamental shift — learning to practice emotional self-reliance, learning to **self-source** what they need for their sense of wholeness and well-being—acknowledging that depending on others for emotional sustenance is as precarious as depending on them for pennies in the room. This points to the necessity of developing emotional self-reliance.

SELF-SOURCING EMOTIONAL NEEDS

The concept of self-sourcing emotional needs can be transformative when understood as replacing dependency with self-reliance, not becoming a closed-hearted "Lone Wolf," and replacing support with isolation. Self-sourcing our emotional needs involves recognizing that we possess an innate capacity to fulfill our needs for security, self-worth, and connection—those are the pennies we already have in our pockets. This does not mean becoming emotionally isolated; it means engaging in relationships not out of necessity but from a place of abundance.

DEVELOPING EMOTIONAL SELF-RELIANCE

Emotional self-reliance is the practice of becoming your primary emotional caretaker. It means nurturing a profound connection with oneself and establishing a sanctuary that no external force can disrupt. This practice diminishes the power others hold over our emotional well-being, effectively neutralizing the root of resentment.

MY ENCOUNTER WITH RESENTMENT

My journey with resentment taught me invaluable lessons about emotional dependency and self-reliance. For years, I harbored resentment towards my wife, feeling unappreciated and undervalued. I was waiting for her to fill the emotional voids within me, to give me the 'pennies' I believed I needed to feel whole.

Through mentorship and reflection, I realized my resentment was a sign of my emotional insolvency. I was expecting my wife to compensate for my internal deficit—an impossible and unfair burden. This realization was pivotal in my journey toward emotional resilience.

TRANSFORMING RESENTMENT INTO RESILIENCE

The path to overcoming resentment begins with a radical reassessment of our emotional dependencies. We must learn a powerful truth - that though someone handed us thirty pennies, we've never needed them. We've always had countless of them in our pockets all along and are free to source our 'pennies' from within rather than seeking them in others. We need to stop believing that we only have what someone gives us. This concept of self-sourcing emotional needs is a foundational shift in transforming our resentment into reconnection. It involves recognizing our innate capacity to fulfill our security, self-worth, and connection needs.

CONCLUSION

Understanding and overcoming resentment requires confronting and often revising our deepest assumptions about emotional fulfillment. By embracing self-reliance and acknowledging our capacity to meet our needs, we free ourselves from the grip of resentment and enhance our ability to form healthier, more fulfilling relationships. The transformation from resentment to resilience is not only profound but entirely achievable, promising a future where our relationships are transformational, marked not by what we can extract from others but by what we can share from a place of emotional abundance.

TWO
BREAKING THE CYCLE OF DEPENDENCY

Dependency often manifests subtly in our relationships, yet it profoundly affects our emotional landscape and the dynamics of our interactions with loved ones. When left unchecked, dependency can foster resentment, diminish self-esteem, and disrupt the balance that is critical for a healthy relationship. In this chapter, I will share with you the steps necessary to break this cycle of dependency and increase your emotional self-sufficiency.

STEP 1: ACKNOWLEDGE THE DEPENDENCY

The first step in overcoming any challenge is acknowledging it exists. In the context of emotional dependency, this means recognizing how you rely on your partner or others to fulfill your emotional needs. It's about understanding that while interdependence is a part of any healthy relationship, over-reliance can lead to vulnerability and dissatisfaction.

STEP 2: UNDERSTAND YOUR EMOTIONAL NEEDS

Once you've acknowledged the presence of dependency, the next step is to understand your deeper emotional needs. This involves introspection and journaling your daily emotional experiences. Ask yourself: What specific needs am I looking to others to fulfill? Am I seeking validation, love, security, or respect from outside sources? By clearly identifying these needs, you can begin to address them independently.

STEP 3: DEVELOP SELF-SOURCING STRATEGIES

To break the cycle of dependency, you must learn to meet your emotional needs from within—a concept I refer to as self-sourcing. This involves developing practices that enhance your sense of self-worth and emotional stability independent of external validation. Techniques such as meditation, self-affirmation, and engaging in fulfilling solo activities can rein-force your emotional independence.

STEP 4: ESTABLISH HEALTHY BOUNDARIES

Setting healthy boundaries is essential for emotional self-sufficiency. This means being able to say no, asking for space when needed, and not feeling guilty for putting your emotional well-being first. Boundaries help you define what you are comfortable with and signal to others how you expect to be treated, supporting a balanced emotional exchange in relationships.

STEP 5: FOSTER EMOTIONAL RESILIENCE

Increasing your emotional resilience is critical in reducing dependency. This means developing the ability to cope with emotional setbacks on your own and not crumbling under pressure or reverting to dependency patterns when faced with relationship challenges. Building resilience can be achieved through practices like cognitive restructuring, where you challenge and change destructive thought patterns.

STEP 6: SEEK SUPPORTIVE RELATIONSHIPS

While working on becoming emotionally self-sufficient, it's also essential to cultivate supportive relationships that encourage your growth. This doesn't contradict the goal of reducing dependency; it enhances your emotional landscape by providing a healthy support network. These relationships should empower you to be your best self without making you feel you owe something in return.

STEP 7: PRACTICE REGULAR REFLECTION

Finally, maintain your progress by engaging in regular reflection. Assess how well you're meeting your emotional needs, the effectiveness of your boundaries, and your overall satisfaction with your relationships. This ongoing evaluation ensures that you stay aligned with your goals of emotional self-sufficiency and can make adjustments as needed.

CONCLUSION

Breaking the cycle of dependency is not about isolating yourself from others but about finding a balance where you can enjoy healthy, supportive relationships without compromising your emotional autonomy. By following these steps, you'll cultivate a stronger, more resilient version of yourself, capable of thriving independently and contributing positively to your relationships.

THREE
THE TYPICAL ANATOMY OF AN UNHAPPY MARRIAGE

In the realm of the struggling marriages I've encountered in my work mentoring men, some common threads are woven through countless narratives of discontent. As a mentor in relationships, I have traversed through the stories of hundreds of men, each bearing the weight of separation, divorce, or the haunting echoes of "I need space." "I love you, but I'm not *in* love with you," and "I'm having an affair." Amidst this diverse tapestry of narratives, I find that a recurring pattern emerges, revealing the anatomy of an unhappy marriage.

UNCOVERING DEEP-SEATED INSECURITY

At first glance, the root cause may not be readily apparent. However, upon closer examination, we unearth a profound sense of insecurity beneath the surface. It's not a blatant declaration of inadequacy that echoes in their minds but rather a pervasive belief that what they seek—validation, connection, or intimacy—is beyond their grasp, sourced externally.

THE ANALOGY OF WATER: UNDERSTANDING DEPENDENCY

To illustrate this concept, consider the analogy of water. Imagine relying on a neighboring property for your water supply. Initially cooperative, this dependency becomes apparent when disagreement strikes, leading to a withdrawal of support. As the source of sustenance falters, so does the trust and reliance placed upon it.

FROM INSECURITY TO DEPENDENCY: THE VICIOUS CYCLE

This dependency breeds neediness, a relentless pursuit of external validation to fill the void within. Like thirsty travelers in a barren land, individuals seek solace in external sources, oblivious to the burgeoning cycle of dependency. With each unmet need, judgment creeps in, followed by blame—a toxic concoction that drives a wedge between partners. Brother, let me tell you —insecurity, neediness, judgment, and blame are the world's worst aphrodisiacs! Yet, this is the vibe many men walk around with. When we live like this, to the woman in our life, it feels like we walk around saying, *"Woman! You displease, disappoint, disgust, and dissatisfy me… can we have more sex? Why don't you want to be with me? I need you to touch my pecker more!"*
It sounds funny and a bit desperate, but this is the exact immature, childish narrative many men live in day after day.

THE MANIFESTATION OF BLAME: A COMMON CASE STUDY

Consider the all-too-familiar scenario of a man fixated on his partner's screen time. Many men tell me their frustration and resentment about how their wife or partner uses her cell phone. Unaware of his insecurity, he scrutinizes her actions, blaming her for his unfulfilled desires. This blame begets resentment, further widening the chasm between them, all while nurturing a narrative of fault and dissatisfaction. "Why won't she put that thing down? Can't she see I have needs?!" I did this too at one time, focusing on my wife's evening reading routine as being a threat to my deep feelings of need for connection, intimacy, and sex. I didn't know it then, but I was experiencing this same pattern.

ESCALATING DISTANCE: THE DISILLUSIONMENT STAGE

As this cycle persists, it propels the relationship into the disillusionment stage, characterized by mutual blame and emotional detachment. Each accusation, each perceived failure, deepens the chasm, fostering an atmosphere of resentment and contempt. This is where most marriages break to total destruction—or total renewal. My personal experience has shown me that when marriage breaks, the thoughts, beliefs, and actions that the man experiences are often (but not always) the key to what happens next.

BREAKING THE CYCLE: THE PATH TO REDEMPTION

While conventional approaches may advocate for mutual introspection, we advocate for a different path. By empowering men to confront their insecurities and reclaim their sense of self-worth, we disrupt the cycle of dependency, ushering in a newfound sense of autonomy and acceptance.

This transformation, though arduous, paves the way for reconciliation and renewal.

CONCLUSION: A GLIMMER OF HOPE

In the landscape of struggling marriages, hope flickers like a distant beacon. By addressing the root cause of insecurity and dependency, we offer a lifeline—a chance for redemption and reconciliation. Through introspection and self-reliance, we navigate the turbulent waters of discontent, guiding couples toward a brighter tomorrow.

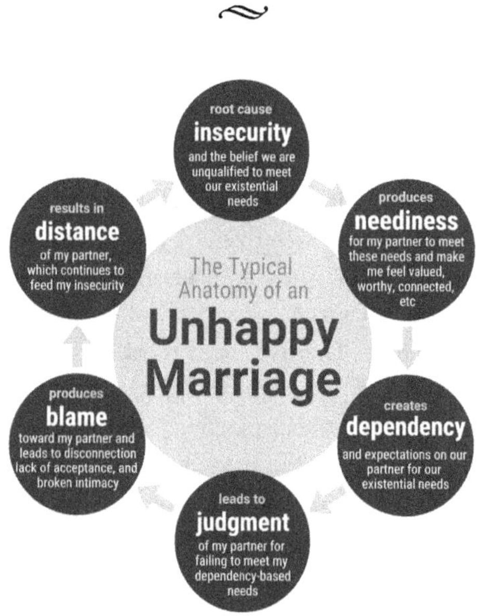

FOUR
THE TYPICAL ANATOMY OF A HAPPY MARRIAGE

The greatest gift you can give your partner is your own happiness.

    — *Esther Hicks*

A symphony of contentment and connection resonates within the sanctuary of a happy marriage. Unlike its somber counterpart, this narrative is imbued with warmth and intimacy, offering a glimpse into the anatomy of marital bliss. You may feel like such a marriage is impossible to experience with your partner, but I promise you, it's not. Many men, including myself, have experienced the depths of resentment, contempt, stonewalling, and disconnection and learned how to lead ourselves and our marriages back to wholeness.

WHOLENESS IS AN INSIDE JOB

Before our marriage can be whole, we must be first. Most men don't walk around proclaiming "I'm not whole" or consciously aware of the deep-seated beliefs about themselves that have led to the formation of their insecurity and dependence. In my work, discovering where we live in feeble stories about our existential needs and where they are met takes several months to uncover. It's a learning process to understand that our emotions are like warning lights, alerting us to things within ourselves that we must look into and address.

When we learn to understand our emotions, look inward, and address areas where we are hurt and wounded, we heal and experience wholeness. That's a process for another book or one you can become intimately acquainted with in my mentoring community.

Understand that your wholeness is a vital first step toward relationship reconnection.

EMBRACING SELF-RELIANCE: A FOUNDATION OF STRENGTH

At the core of a thriving marriage lies a profound sense of emotional self-reliance—a recognition that one's worth and fulfillment stem from within. Of course, we cannot experience this if we don't first experience the wholeness above. However, once healed, we break our old patterns of seeking external validation, and we learn to embrace our inherent value, worth, and significance, fostering a strengthening sense of wholeness and completeness.

FROM DEPENDENCY TO OPENNESS: A PARADIGM SHIFT

This completeness changes everything. Dim becomes the painful shackles of dependency, replaced by an ethos of looking within. The natural result —is openness and acceptance. As we are freed from the burden of expectation, we begin to revel in each other's presence, unencumbered by judgment or blame. This newfound sense of liberation fosters an environment of mutual respect and understanding. We stop focusing on how our partner disappoints us and begin to see what we admire and appreciate.

CULTIVATING WARMTH AND GENEROSITY: THE RIPPLE EFFECT

In the absence of neediness and manipulation, warmth and generosity flourish. We begin to bask in the radiance of genuine affection, secure in the knowledge that our worth is not contingent upon external validation. This abundance mentality permeates every facet of their relationship, creating a virtuous cycle of love and reciprocity.

This wholly and utterly changes the former transaction-based, commercial exchanges of giving to get that formerly characterized our relationship. Trade is supplanted by generosity, benevolence, compassion, and sharing. This letting go of mutual neediness breeds perhaps one of the most liberating relationship qualities —freedom. We're each free to be genuinely ourselves.

EMBRACING VULNERABILITY: THE KEY TO INTIMACY

This freedom and vulnerability reign supreme within the confines of a happy marriage. Partners shed their masks, baring their souls to one another without fear of judgment or rejection. This raw authenticity forms the bedrock of intimacy, fostering a profound connection that transcends the superficial. I didn't honestly know intimacy until this aspect of my marriage. Had you told me the best intimacy of my marriage would happen after several decades, I would have guffawed and looked at you like you were crazy. Yet, this is the case!

Freedom to be ourselves creates epic vulnerability, which becomes the basis for white-hot, deeply satisfying connection and intimacy.

NAVIGATING CHALLENGES: A UNIFIED FRONT

Even amidst life's inevitable challenges, the bond forged in a happy marriage remains unyielding —so long as you continue each day to create it. Unified in purpose and resolve and confident in one another's capacity to take care of themselves while being available for support, partners can face adversity hand in hand, drawing strength from their unwavering commitment to one another. Through communication, compromise, and steadfast support, they weather the storm together, emerging more robust and resilient.

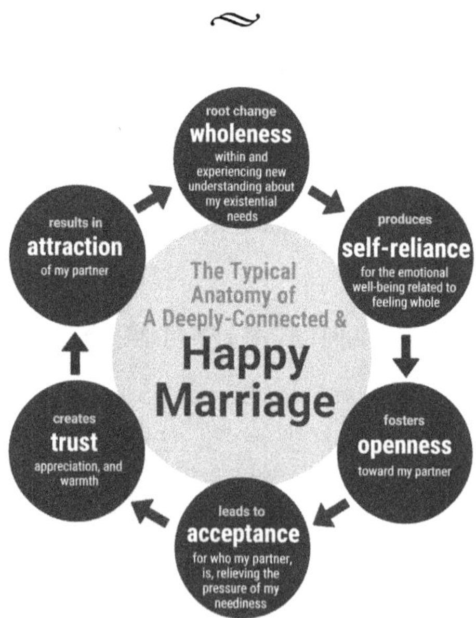

FIVE

NAVIGATING FROM RESENTMENT TO CONNECTION

A human being is a part of the whole called by us universe, a part limited in time and space. He experiences himself, his thoughts and feeling as something separated from the rest, a kind of optical delusion of his consciousness. This delusion is a kind of prison for us, restricting us to our personal desires and to affection for a few persons nearest to us. Our task must be to free ourselves from this prison by widening our circle of compassion to embrace all living creatures and the whole of nature in its beauty.

—*Albert Einstein*

As we journey through the landscape of personal and marital challenges, understanding how to transition from insecurity, dependency, and resentment to connection is crucial. This chapter sets the stage for a deeper dive into the principles that have transformed my life and the lives of many men I mentor. While we'll explore these principles in detail in Part II of this book, let me briefly introduce them as they are the stepping stones from the emotional quagmire of resentment to the solid ground of connected, fulfilling relationships.

INTRODUCTION TO THE FOUR KEYS

My path from resentment, and the one I've led many men through, involves more than just overcoming negative emotions; it requires building a new foundation based on four key principles: Unconditional High Regard, Ownership, Self-Reliance, and Brotherhood. Each of these plays a crucial role in healing ourselves, relationships, and personal growth and development. In the following chapter, I will share personal stories and insights that delve deeply into each of these principles, explaining how they have facilitated profound changes in my life and the lives of others.

UNCONDITIONAL HIGH REGARD

Unconditional High Regard is about seeing the inherent value in others, even when conflicts arise. It's a principle that promotes empathy and understanding, crucial for transcending resentment.

OWNERSHIP

Ownership focuses on taking responsibility for our emotions and reactions. It's about shifting from a mindset of blame to one of proactive personal accountability.

SELF-RELIANCE

Self-reliance encourages us to fulfill our own emotional

needs, reducing dependency on others and thereby mitigating resentment that stems from unmet expectations.

BROTHERHOOD

Brotherhood entails forming supportive relationships with other men who are committed to emotional health and mutual growth. This network is invaluable for sustaining the changes we make.

TRANSITION TO PART II

As we conclude this introductory discussion, we stand on the threshold of a deeper exploration. In Part II of this book, I will expound on these four keys in detail. We will examine how each principle can be applied to not only navigate away from resentment but to also build a life characterized by robust emotional health and enriched relationships. This journey is about laying down the burdens of the past and picking up the tools for a healthier, more connected future.

PART TWO
UNDERSTANDING THE FOUR KEYS

Until you make the unconscious conscious, it will direct your life and you will call it fate.
— Carl Jung

SIX
EMBRACING UNCONDITIONAL HIGH REGARD

Out beyond ideas of wrongdoing and rightdoing, there is a field. I'll meet you there.
> *— Rumi*

≈

Unconditional High Regard was the first key I discovered on my path to recovery, and it challenged everything I thought I knew about love and respect in a relationship. If you've ever wondered how a single change in perspective can revolutionize your entire life, let me take you through how this principle became the cornerstone of my journey from resentment to resilience.

UNDERSTANDING UNCONDITIONAL HIGH REGARD

Unconditional High Regard meant accepting and appreciating Zelda for what she did that pleased me and for who she was, regardless of her actions. It was about seeing the value in her, independent of my judgments and expectations. The concept was simple yet profound: value and respect others not for what they do but for what and *who* they are. This doesn't mean you approve of everything they do; it means their inherent worth as human beings does not fluctuate based on their actions toward me.

EARLY ATTEMPTS AND CHALLENGES

Adopting this mindset was not easy. My initial attempts were clumsy, often faltering under the strain of old habits. There were times when my efforts seemed futile when the old resentments threatened to resurface. Yet, each time I chose to view Zelda with unconditional regard, the walls between us softened slightly. I used to think Zelda needed to earn my respect and kindness through her actions and words. If she did something I appreciated, I would be warm and loving. If she did something that irked me, the cold shoulder was hers. This was conditional regard—my affection and respect depended on her meeting my expectations.

To be precise, and many people misunderstand this, unconditional high regard is not an unconditional relationship. Relationships, especially marriage, are innately conditional. This is about recognizing what regard a person is worthy of despite being in a relationship with me.

I struggled with this initially because I had a very conditional regard for myself. I was harsh toward myself and had suffered from self-loathing for decades. My regard for myself will ultimately become the ceiling of my regard for others. I'd been fooling myself for years, thinking that I could love and value someone more deeply than I do myself, but now I see that such gestures were just manipulative acts to gain their attention, approval, validation, and love.

FINDING A DEEPER SENSE OF VALUE

Through this practice, I began recognizing my intrinsic value and worth, separate from how others responded. This journey led me to a deeper understanding of self-worth that was not contingent on external validation. I realized that my feelings of inadequacy were tied to my perception of how Zelda and others treated me and founded on an underlying belief that other people and how they feel about me determine my value and worth. But it's called "self-worth," not "others-worth!" Yet, somehow, this had escaped my notice all my life.

Focusing on unconditional regard and what it meant to express it to myself, I started to detach my self-esteem from these external influences. I discovered a more stable and profound sense of self-worth that continues to become increasingly unshakeable with time.

A TRANSFORMATIVE ANNIVERSARY AND ROUGH PATCHES

One significant test of this new approach came during our 25th wedding anniversary. Instead of expecting Zelda to meet my unspoken desires for the day, I focused on appreciating our time together, whatever the outcome. This shift in perspective transformed what might have been a day of disappointment into one of genuine connection and joy.

The real test of my commitment to unconditional high regard came during a particularly stressful period for Zelda involving homeschooling and a passion project. This would have led to weeks of silent battles and hidden resentment. This time, I leaned into unconditional high regard. I listened more, offered support without conditions, and, importantly, withheld judgment.

THE POWER OF UNCONDITIONAL HIGH REGARD

This new approach didn't solve our problems overnight but fundamentally changed how we tackled them. Discussions that might have turned into arguments became conversations and even opportunities for connection. Moments that could have spiraled into emotional chaos became opportunities for mutual support. The shift was initially subtle—a slight ease in the tension, a smoother flow to our conversations. It wasn't that Zelda suddenly changed; I had transformed. By adopting unconditional high regard, I stopped tallying faults. I started appreciating our interactions for what they were—complex, sometimes messy, but always shared moments between two people doing their best. Unconditional High Regard involves giving one another the benefit of the doubt.

Looking back, the transformation seems miraculous, but it wasn't magic—it was a deliberate choice, repeated day after day. Unconditional high regard saved my marriage because it first saved me from my cycle of conditional self-love, judgment, shame, and silent scorekeeping that creates resentment and contempt.

As we move forward, remember this: the power of unconditional high regard can be your foundation, too. It starts with a choice, a simple shift in perspective that says, "I choose to see value in this person, no matter what." Stick with me, and I'll show you how this key and the others can unlock a life of deeper connection and genuine happiness.

SEVEN

TAKING OWNERSHIP

I am not a product of my circumstances. I am a product of my decisions.

— *Stephen R. Covey*

Ownership became the second transformative key in my journey, reshaping my marriage and my entire life approach. This chapter explores how embracing full responsibility for my feelings, actions, and our relationship dynamics led to profound changes.

For over twenty years of marriage, I'd grown into an absolute expert at seeing Zelda, others, and external circumstances as the source of all my pain, frustration, and disappointment. I'd always considered myself somewhat pious because I hadn't verbalized my hard feelings to Zelda much and kept my mouth shut. Yet, inwardly, I was an Olympic Gold Medalist at blame, a total "nice guy," going along to get along and withholding my true feelings. In a word, I was immature.

THE CONCEPT OF OWNERSHIP

Ownership meant ceasing to blame Zelda or anyone else for my unhappiness and no longer waiting passively for things to improve. It represented a profound internal shift from viewing myself as a victim of circumstances to being the master of my fate. This shift was about moving from blame and passivity to proactive engagement and empowerment.

OWNING MY NARRATIVE

The power of owning my narrative became evident during a session with my coach, who challenged me to reframe my story. For years, I had cast Zelda as the antagonist, the source of my discontent. I had always labeled her "adversarial," and she seemed to me to be contentious as a "nice," easy-going guy, which bugged me.

Steve, my coach, posed a critical question that other men close to me also began to ask: "What if Zelda isn't the problem? What if the way you're seeing your story is?"

This question catalyzed a significant transformation. I realized that I dodged responsibility for my feelings and actions whenever I positioned Zelda as the villain. I decided to rewrite my internal script. Instead of a narrative in which I was the victim of Zelda's shortcomings, I chose a story in which I was the hero of my growth, fully responsible for my happiness and fulfillment. This allowed me to stop feeling like I had no choices or power and begin feeling relief from the hard emotions blame gave birth to - anger, frustration, resentment, and contempt.

OWNING MY EMOTIONS

A critical aspect of ownership is managing one's emotions. I recall an evening when Zelda and I disagreed about weekend plans and felt my anger rising. Instead of succumbing to old habits of blame, I paused and asked myself, "What part of this is mine to own?"

The answer was clear: my reaction. Rather than lashing out, I owned my frustration and chose to express it constructively. I explained to Zelda, "I'm feeling frustrated because I was looking forward to our plans, and it seems we're not aligning. I find myself wanting to blame you, but I know my emotions are mine to sort through." This approach didn't just prevent escalation—it kept me open-hearted and connected and opened a dialogue that led to us finding a solution, maintaining peace, and fostering deeper understanding.

I always thought that connection came from telling other people my thoughts and emotions and getting them to agree with me and see life the same way. So, I spent much time explaining myself, re-explaining myself, arguing, defending, and hating being misunderstood. This never seemed to lead to deep emotional connection and intimacy; it eroded it.

As I learned how to take ownership of my emotions, I continued to share them when it made sense but stopped trying to get Zelda or others to fix them. This relieved a lot of pressure, and with the removal of my expectations of them for their response came a natural acceptance of them as they are. As I stopped needing her to be responsible for my emotional state, she experienced more freedom and desire to come toward me and connect more intimately, and our relationship strengthened.

OWNING MY ACTIONS

Ownership also extends to one's actions and their impact on others. A turning point for me was recognizing how my passivity or inaction contributed to issues in our marriage. I had often been passive, expecting Zelda to fulfill my needs intuitively. During a family vacation, which previously might have been ripe for conflict, I proactively communicated with Zelda about my expectations and listened to hers. This mutual ownership of our vacation plans led to one of our most enjoyable trips, free from the undercurrents of unspoken resentments.

FACING THE TRUTH

In my journey of transforming my marriage with Zelda, I realized that for many years, I had been treating our relationship like a rental property rather than a home I owned. At first, this analogy seems unusual, but it perfectly encapsulates the shift in mindset necessary for our relationship to thrive.

Initially, I approached our marriage like a tenant, not an owner. I was there, yes, physically present, but I wasn't fully committed to the deep, ongoing maintenance the relationship required. Like a renter who might not bother fixing a leaky faucet because it's not "their problem," I avoided addressing deeper issues between us. If problems got too bothersome, I hoped they would resolve themselves, or Zelda would do something about them. This detachment allowed me to avoid taking real responsibility; I was emotionally guarded, investing just enough to keep things running but not enough to improve or deeply connect with Zelda.

But there came a point when I realized that this approach was unsustainable. The turning point was subtle, not marked by any grand event, but rather a series of small, quiet acknowledgments to myself about the kind of life and marriage I truly wanted. I asked myself, "What if I truly owned this relationship? What if I stopped waiting for Zelda to make the first move or to fix things? What if I started investing as if I were meant to be here forever?"

EMBRACING OWNERSHIP MEANT A RADICAL SHIFT.

It meant actively participating in the upkeep and growth of our marriage, much like a homeowner who invests in their property. It meant painting walls—not just patching them—planting a garden, not just mowing the lawn. It meant nurturing and caring for my relationship with Zelda with the intention of permanence and beauty.

I began to address issues directly, communicate more openly, and show up fully as a partner and co-creator of our shared life. I started to repair the emotional damage between us, initiate meaningful conversations, and, most crucially, invest in understanding and meeting Zelda's and my support needs.

This mindset of ownership transformed our marriage. It wasn't quick or easy—like any renovation, it took time, effort, and sometimes, going back to the drawing board. But gradually, our relationship became less like a temporary arrangement and more like a cherished home. We both felt more secure, valued, and deeply connected.

Adopting this approach taught me that steadfast commitment in a marriage is about more than staying together. It's about how deeply you're willing to invest in and care for the relationship, not as a mere participant but as a dedicated, proactive owner. This realization wasn't just about taking responsibility; it was about embracing the joy and the work of building a life together that is truly our own.

CONCLUSION

Through these experiences, I learned that ownership isn't just about taking responsibility; it's about liberation. Every moment of ownership was a step away from the old, resentful patterns and toward a more satisfying and connected life. These chapters lay the groundwork for the profound changes that followed. Each key built on the last, leading to a deeper understanding and transformation of my marriage and myself.

As we close this chapter on ownership, remember that it is a key that unlocks more than just personal growth or marital harmony; it unlocks a deeper engagement with life itself. As we proceed to the following key, remember that each step of taking ownership paves the way for even more significant changes. Let's continue our journey to self-reliance, exploring the power of finding strength and answers within ourselves.

EIGHT

CULTIVATING SELF-RELIANCE

Trust thyself: every heart vibrates to that iron string.
— *Ralph Waldo Emerson*

∿

Cultivating self-reliance wasn't just an epiphany in my adult years; its seeds were sown in my childhood's fertile, albeit rocky, soil. Growing up, I learned to rely on myself in empowering and, at times, profoundly isolating ways. This chapter is about how I applied self-reliance in my marriage and how these early experiences shaped my understanding of what it means to be self-reliant.

EARLY LESSONS IN INDEPENDENCE

My journey towards self-reliance began much earlier than I often acknowledge. As a child, I learned quickly that waiting for someone else to fix things or to provide comfort usually ended in disappointment. Whether repairing a broken toy or dealing with schoolyard bullies, I learned to fend for myself. This independence was a double-edged sword; it crafted a resilience in me from a young age but also ingrained a deep-seated belief that I must go it alone, that relying on others was a gamble not worth taking.

DYSFUNCTIONAL FOUNDATIONS

This formative independence, however, was not without its dysfunctional aspects. I recall a pivotal incident when I was about twelve. Our family lawn tractor broke down, and instead of my father handling the situation, he handed it off to me, saying, "See what you can do, son." I was twelve—a child with no mechanical knowledge. Yet, there I was, trying to figure out an engine because I believed no one else would or could help (and I was successful!).

This scenario repeated itself in various forms throughout my youth, reinforcing the idea that I was my only reliable resource. This belief followed me into adulthood and into my marriage, where it initially manifested as a refusal to seek support and ask others for help or to share my vulnerabilities genuinely.

A TURNING POINT IN PUERTO VALLARTA

A pivotal moment in my journey toward genuine self-reliance unfolded under the warm sun of Puerto Vallarta. This wasn't about learning to change my oil or fix every household issue, though those skills have their place. My revelation in Mexico was about a deeper, more profound form of self-reliance rooted in identity rather than mere capability.

Being in Puerto Vallarta, away from the daily grind and usual responsibilities, I reflected deeply on self-reliance. It struck me that genuine self-reliance wasn't about doing more but being more. This realization came as I walked along the beach one morning, the waves echoing the tumultuous thoughts that had long filled my mind.

In the past, I'd often looked externally for validation, support, and happiness—whether from Zelda, my career, or even my community. I had always thought I would feel complete if I could achieve enough, provide enough, or be recognized as sufficient. But standing there, with the vast ocean in front of me, I understood that what I needed was to find those things within myself.

This form of self-reliance I was discovering was based on being. It was about acknowledging and embracing the completeness of my being without seeking external affirmation. It required a profound internal shift—recognizing that I lack nothing and that my value doesn't diminish based on circumstances or others' perceptions.

With this mindset, I began to see that self-reliance is the natural outcome of truly valuing oneself. It's about understanding that my origin is in being, not becoming or achieving. This perspective liberated me from relentlessly pursuing external solutions for my internal voids.

During my time in Puerto Vallarta, as I continued to explore this new understanding, I realized how my previous view of self-reliance had often led to unnecessary strain in my marriage. I had burdened Zelda with the impossible task of fulfilling needs that were, in truth, mine to satisfy. This misplacement of responsibility fueled many of our conflicts and my frustrations.

Armed with this new insight, I returned home committed to applying this principle of identity-based self-reliance to our relationship. I focused less on doing as a strategy to earn love or respect and more on being a complete person in my own right. This shift didn't just change how I interacted with Zelda; it transformed the very foundation of our interactions. Discussions that might have once spiraled into blame or resentment now became opportunities for genuine connection and mutual support.

This change was not instant, and it certainly wasn't easy. But as I practiced being self-reliant in this new way—focusing on my inner completeness and reducing my reliance on external validation—our marriage began to reflect this newfound health and wholeness. It became clear that every relationship is transformed positively when one is genuinely self-reliant in the most profound and authentic sense.

This journey in Puerto Vallarta wasn't just a retreat but a turning point—a profound shift from seeking to being, from external reliance to internal fulfillment. It taught me that the most vital foundation for any relationship is not found in what we can do for each other but in being whole and complete within ourselves, thus enabling us to engage with each other from a place of fullness, not lack.

TRANSFORMING MY MARRIAGE THROUGH SELF-RELIANCE

Back home, with a new understanding of self-reliance, I approached my relationship with Zelda differently. During an agitated period, I remembered the lessons from my youth—not the lesson to isolate, but to handle what I could and to share what I couldn't. I started owning my part in our conflicts and managing my reactions, but I also opened up about my struggles and asked for her support when needed. This balance transformed our interactions from a series of transactions to a partnership built on mutual support and understanding.

THE BROADER IMPACT

As I embraced this more profound, more authentic form of self-reliance, the impact extended far beyond my sense of fulfillment and directly influenced every aspect of my life, particularly my relationships.

Understanding that self-reliance is about being rather than doing shifted how I interacted with Zelda and engaged with the world around me. This newfound perspective allowed me to approach life with completeness and confidence that wasn't contingent on external validation or achievements. It was liberating to realize that my worth wasn't tied to my productivity or the approval of others but rather to the inherent value I possess simply by being.

This shift profoundly affected my role as husband, father, and leader. I became more present and grounded at home, no longer seeking Zelda's constant approval to affirm my identity. This change reduced the pressure within our marriage, allowing for more authentic and less transactional interactions. Our home became a place of mutual respect and understanding where we could thrive in our true selves.

Professionally, this approach transformed my interactions with colleagues and clients. I approached my work with a steadier hand and a clearer mind, no longer driven by the frantic need to prove myself. This not only improved my performance but also fostered a healthier work environment. I led with empathy and focused on collective well-being, enhancing my team's morale and productivity.

I noticed a shift in how I was perceived in the broader community. People began to respond to the calm confidence that now characterized my interactions. This wasn't the result of any deliberate effort to impress or dominate but came naturally from my internal self-reliance. I found that people were more drawn to this genuine presentation than they had been to my previous, more effortful persona.

Perhaps most importantly, this journey into self-reliance deepened my connections with my children. By embodying this principle, I taught them—more through actions than words—that their worth is inherent and not dependent on external achievements or recognition. This has encouraged them to pursue their interests and relationships with a sense of security and self-assuredness.

The broader impact of embracing identity-based self-reliance has been a life characterized by deeper connections, reduced stress, and a genuine sense of peace and content-ment. It taught me that the most profound strength comes not from what we do but from who we are at our core. As I continue to live out these principles, I see the ripples extending outward, influencing others to consider where their sense of self-reliance might lead them.

This transformation is not just a personal victory; it's a beacon for anyone seeking to redefine their interactions and life's path. Through this book, I aim to inspire others to discover the power of self-reliance that originates from within, fostering a life of authenticity and profound connection.

CONCLUSION

Reflecting on the full spectrum of my experiences with self-reliance—from the dysfunctional lessons of my youth to the empowering revelations of adulthood—I've come to under-stand that self-reliance isn't about going it alone. It's about being secure in your abilities and open to the contributions of others. As we move forward to the next chapter on Brother-hood, we'll explore how the lessons of self-reliance inform and enrich our relationships with fellow men.

NINE

BROTHERHOOD – THE CIRCLE OF STRENGTH

If you want to go fast, go alone. If you want to go far, go together.

    — African Proverb

My understanding of brotherhood began in isolation, shadowed by a longing for genuine connection. During one of my lowest points, feeling the weight of loneliness, I stumbled upon the concept of brotherhood as more than camaraderie—a profound support system. A turning point came when I reached out to Steve, the men's coach who appeared in a video that spoke directly to my struggles. His invitation to join a community of like-minded men was my first step toward a transformative alliance.

THE FIRST GATHERING: A MEETING OF MINDS AND HEARTS

I'll never forget my first meeting with this group of men. As we sat nervously in a Zoom meeting, each sharing our journeys and the burdens we carried, I felt a collective strength that was both uplifting and grounding. This was not about friendship but building a sanctuary where vulnerabilities could be shared without judgment. Each story added to the fabric of our collective resilience.

THE POWER OF SHARED STRUGGLES

The true power of brotherhood revealed itself as we tackled personal challenges together. Whether it was a marriage in turmoil, a career at a crossroads, or a personal crisis, the group's insights and support provided clarity and courage. For me, the realization that I was not alone in my struggles was liberating. Each session with these men taught me that shared burdens are halved while shared joys are doubled.

SUPPORT BEYOND WORDS

One particularly poignant experience was when a member of our group, John, faced a personal tragedy. The way the group rallied around him, offering emotional support and practical help and resources, exemplified the essence of brotherhood. During this time, I truly understood the impact of having a brotherhood—it was about showing up, not just during the meetings, but in real life.

ONGOING ENGAGEMENT AND GROWTH

Maintaining this bond required commitment. We established regular check-ins, retreats, and social gatherings to strengthen our forged connection. Through this ongoing engagement, we all continued to grow, influenced by each other's perspectives and experiences. The brotherhood became a cornerstone of my personal development and remains integral, reminding me that growth is not just a solitary journey but a communal voyage.

THE BROADER IMPACT OF BROTHERHOOD

The ripple effects of this brotherhood extended beyond our own lives. As we became calmer, powerful, and resilient, we became better husbands, fathers, and community leaders. The principles we practiced—unconditional support, honest communication, and mutual respect—became tools we each took into our worlds, spreading the impact of what we had learned and experienced together.

I went on to create Masterful Men (https://become.master ful.men), a global men's mentoring community dedicated to helping men navigate difficult circumstances like the ones that brought us together. I'll share more about Masterful Men with you in later chapters.

A CALL TO BROTHERHOOD

This chapter of my story is an invitation to every man feeling the pangs of isolation or the crush of unshared burdens. Brotherhood, I've learned, is vital for personal resilience and collective empowerment. It's a call to move beyond superficial relationships and engage in a fellowship that transforms lives. If you're seeking to survive and thrive, the path of brotherhood is waiting. If you think you can do it alone, you're fooling yourself. I'd suggest that a man is unlikely to implement the former three keys well without Brotherhood. Men need transformation more than information; the best way to experience transformation is to be around others experiencing it.

PART THREE
APPLYING THE FOUR KEYS IN LIFE AND MARRIAGE

An unexamined life is not worth living. — Socrates

TEN
INTEGRATING THE KEYS – A LIFE TRANSFORMED

As we explore the interplay between Unconditional High Regard, Ownership, Self-Reliance, and Brotherhood, we see that these concepts aren't just individual pillars but interwoven strands that together create a sturdy net capable of catching us in times of personal crisis and elevating our daily experiences.

SYNERGIZING GROWTH: MORE THAN THE SUM OF ITS PARTS

Think of these keys as ingredients in a life-changing recipe. Each one is essential and enhances the others:

- **Unconditional High Regard** is about seeing the

inherent value in others and ourselves, regardless of circumstances.

- **Ownership** means accepting responsibility for our actions and their impacts.
- **Self-reliance** involves trusting in our abilities and decisions.
- **Brotherhood** represents the strength and support we find in communal bonds.

When mixed, these elements create a dynamic and thriving life. Each component stands strong and complements and strengthens the others, leading to exponential personal and relational growth.

EMPATHETIC ACCOUNTABILITY: COMBINING UNCONDITIONAL HIGH REGARD AND OWNERSHIP

By blending Unconditional High Regard with Ownership, I've nurtured a practice I call 'Empathetic Accountability.' This approach allows me to resolve conflicts with compassion and responsibility, turning potential barriers into bridges for deeper understanding and connection.

SUPPORTED INDEPENDENCE: THE UNION OF SELF-RELIANCE AND BROTHERHOOD

The combination of Self-Reliance and Brotherhood fosters 'Supported Independence.' This concept shows that individual strength is maximized through community support, demonstrating that true independence thrives in isolation and within a supportive network.

INTEGRATING ALL KEYS: A MULTIFACETED APPROACH TO LIFE'S CHALLENGES

When life throws challenges our way, utilizing all four keys together equips us with a comprehensive toolkit. This integrated approach ensures that we face adversity with resilience and a proactive strategy for growth. Whether personal setbacks, professional difficulties, or relationship issues, this holistic method helps transform challenges into opportunities for significant growth.

THE RIPPLE EFFECT: HOW INTEGRATION CHANGES EVERYTHING

The synergy of these keys transforms more than just individual lives; it initiates a wave of positive change that influences all aspects of our existence. This ripple effect reaches our families, workplaces, and communities, creating a legacy of enriched interactions, purposeful living, and inspired leadership.

THE CONTINUUM OF GROWTH: A LIFELONG JOURNEY

As we wrap up this discussion, remember that personal transformation is a never-ending journey. The framework of these four keys is not just for today's challenges but serves as a lifelong guide to personal fulfillment and community involvement. Keep these principles in mind, apply them conscientiously, and welcome each new day as an opportunity to live intentionally, connect deeply, and have a broad impact.

Together, with these principles in hand, we are well-equipped to navigate the complexities of life. This journey is ongoing; every step forward enriches our existence and extends our influence.

ELEVEN

LIVING THE LESSONS – EVERYDAY APPLICATIONS

When we are no longer able to change a situation, we are challenged to change ourselves.
— Viktor E. Frankl

This chapter delves into the practical day-to-day applications of the four foundational keys: Unconditional High Regard, Ownership, Self-Reliance, and Brotherhood. It shows how these principles can seamlessly integrate into everyday experiences, transforming routine interactions and enhancing life's pivotal moments.

CULTIVATE A DAILY PRACTICE OF UNCONDITIONAL HIGH REGARD

Practicing Unconditional High Regard daily means actively seeing the intrinsic worth in everyone I encounter. It starts with the morning greetings to my children and neighbors, continues with things like a respectful nod or curious inquiry to the barista or cashiers, and extends to listening attentively to my family members' day. Each interaction is an opportunity to affirm someone's value, which enriches my relationships and deepens connections. This practice teaches me to consistently act with kindness and patience, even in challenging circumstances, thereby fostering a more compassionate community around me.

BEGIN EMBRACING ACCOUNTABILITY

Every day is filled with moments when I can exercise ownership. Whether it's a work-related error or a misstep in my personal life, I strive to acknowledge my part. This commitment to Ownership means actively apologizing when necessary, offering solutions when problems arise, and stepping forward to make amends. This approach clears misunderstandings, strengthens my integrity, and builds trust with those around me.

INTEGRATE SELF-RELIANCE IN YOUR ROUTINE

Self-reliance permeates my daily life, encouraging me to take initiative and rely on my skills and judgment. From managing finances to making health-related decisions, I rely on my internal compass to guide me. This key empowers me to trust my instincts, learn new skills, and solve problems independently, which boosts my confidence and ensures I am not overly dependent on others for my happiness or well-being.

CREATE BROTHERHOOD IN EVERYDAY RELATIONSHIPS

While my men's community, Masterful Men, provides a robust support system, the essence of Brotherhood influences all my relationships. I aim to offer empathy, support, and accountability to my neighbors, colleagues, friends, and family, mirroring the camaraderie of the group. This broad application of Brotherhood enriches my relationships, creating a solid mutual support network that transcends traditional boundaries and enhances communal well-being.

LEVERAGE GROWTH FROM EVERYDAY STRUGGLES

Life's daily grind comes with its share of challenges, each presenting a unique opportunity to apply these transformative keys. Whether facing a technical glitch at work or a personal conflict, I utilize Ownership and Self-Reliance to address issues head-on while employing Unconditional High Regard and Brotherhood to maintain positive, supportive interactions. These principles transform potential obstacles into valuable growth opportunities, enhancing my resilience and adaptability.

CRAFT A FULFILLING DAILY EXPERIENCE

Integrating these keys into daily life has improved my approach to challenges and enhanced my capacity to enjoy and celebrate life's joys. These principles encourage a richer, more engaged experience of the world, prompting me to appreciate the moment, value the people in my life, and contribute positively to my community. They transform ordinary days into a dynamic practice of personal development and fulfillment.

FINAL THOUGHTS

As we conclude this chapter, I invite you to weave these keys into your daily routine. Start with small, manageable actions, maintain consistency, and observe as the principles that have profoundly shaped my life begin to enrich yours. Each day offers a fresh opportunity to paint your life's canvas with broader strokes of growth, joy, and fulfillment.

However, don't expect instantaneous results or that acquiring new information is all it takes to experience profound transformation. Be patient and kind with yourself, and expect your transformation to take diligence, effort, and time. Though it may feel urgent to experience these changes, they rarely are. Instead of seeking a more comfortable and certain future, focus on improving your present and being the best version of yourself until bedtime. Then, do that again tomorrow.

TWELVE

EXPANDING THE IMPACT – SHARING THE KEYS WITH OTHERS

First say to yourself what you would be; and then do what you have to do.

> — *Epictetus*

A man's growth is never done. There is no finish line, and as my coach and mentor, Steve Horsmon, used to tell me, "This work is climbing a mountain with no top." We must learn to enjoy the journey for what it is.

One of the most potent ways men experience transformation, a force multiplier, is to begin sharing the changes we're experiencing with others.

The transformative journey doesn't just stop with personal growth and improved relationships; it begins. All living things reproduce. A man alive naturally extends the life within him, sharing these powerful principles with others, thereby amplifying the impact and creating a legacy of change.

TEACHING BY EXAMPLE

One of the most profound ways I've shared the principles of Unconditional High Regard, Ownership, Self-Reliance, and Brotherhood is by embodying these values consistently. By living these keys, we serve as a model for others, whether consciously or subconsciously, imparting these lessons to our family, friends, and strangers. This form of teaching by example is powerful because it demonstrates the practical benefits of these principles in real-life contexts, inspiring others to adopt similar approaches.

WORKSHOPS, COURSES, AND MENTORING

Beyond informal modeling, some men will take a more direct approach by developing workshops and coaching or mentoring programs. These structured environments provide a platform for men to share the keys in a formal setting, guiding others through the concepts and practices that have reshaped my life. Through my interactive courses, I've engaged with individuals and groups, providing them with the tools and support they need to embark on their journeys of transformation. You can do the same!

WRITING, SPEAKING & DIGITAL OUTREACH

Writing articles, blog posts, and, eventually, this book has been a crucial method of sharing the principles I've learned. Each piece of written content reaches a different audience, spreading the message of transformation far beyond my immediate circle. Additionally, speaking engagements at conferences, community events, and seminars have allowed me to vocalize my journey and the lessons I've learned, touching lives in diverse communities and sparking conversations about change and growth.

Now, I invite you to take part in this transformative journey. By engaging with these ideas, whether through reading, discussing them with others, or applying them in your own life, you, too, can become an agent of change. I encourage you to share your insights and experiences through your writings, social media, or conversations with friends and family. Each interaction offers a chance to influence others positively and extend the ripple effect of transformation initiated by your personal growth.

PERSONAL CONNECTIONS

While broad outreach has its place, the deep, one-on-one connections remain profoundly impactful. I seize opportunities to share insights from my journey through coaching sessions, casual coffee meetings, or even casual conversations. These personal engagements allow for tailored discussions where I can address specific challenges and provide detailed guidance on applying the keys in individual contexts.

LIVING A LIFE OF INFLUENCE

The journey of transformation is not just about improving oneself but also about enriching the lives of others. Each conversation, each piece of advice, and each shared story has the potential to initiate a chain reaction of growth and change. As this chapter concludes, consider how you might share your journey and insights with others. Embrace the role of mentor, teacher, and friend, and watch as the principles that have transformed your life begin to light sparks of change in others.

As we move forward, remember that each of us has the potential to be a catalyst for transformation, not just in our lives but in the world around us. Let's carry forward the commitment to live by these keys and pass them on, expanding the impact and creating a lasting legacy of positivity and growth.

THIRTEEN
FACING FORWARD –
CONTINUING THE JOURNEY OF
GROWTH

Do not go where the path may lead, go instead where there is no path and leave a trail.
  — *Ralph Waldo Emerson*

～

Now it's time to look towards the future, contemplating the continued application of the principles we've embraced and considering how to maintain momentum in our transformative journey, even as life's circumstances evolve.

EMBRACING LIFELONG LEARNING

The journey of personal transformation is perpetual. It doesn't end with achieving goals or mastering certain principles—it continues as long as we are committed to growth. Embracing lifelong learning involves staying curious, seeking new knowledge, and being open to revisiting and refining the four keys as life unfolds. This mindset ensures that we remain adaptable and responsive to new challenges and opportunities for growth.

BUILDING RESILIENCE

Life is unpredictable, and challenges are inevitable. Building resilience is crucial for sustaining our changes and facing future adversities without reverting to old patterns. Resilience involves enduring difficult times and using them as catalysts for further growth. By applying the principles of Ownership and Self-Reliance during tough times, we can strengthen our ability to cope with and thrive through life's inevitable ups and downs.

DEEPENING RELATIONSHIPS

As we move forward, our focus should also include deepening the relationships our journey has transformed. This means going beyond surface-level interactions and fostering genuine connections rooted in Unconditional High Regard and Brotherhood. It's about continuously nurturing these relationships, making space for vulnerability, and supporting others in their growth just as we seek their support.

EXPANDING OUR INFLUENCE

With the profound personal changes we've experienced, it's natural to want to share these gifts with others. Expanding our influence might involve mentoring others, participating in community leadership, or advocating for positive change in everyday interactions. Each act of sharing has the potential to influence others' lives positively, further multiplying the impact of the journey we've embarked on.

RENEWING OUR COMMITMENT

We must periodically renew our commitment by setting new goals to keep our journey dynamic and engaging. These goals should challenge us to apply the keys in new ways and areas of our lives. Whether improving a professional skill, nurturing a new hobby, or enhancing a relationship, each new goal gives us a fresh direction for applying our learning and keeping our journey vibrant and rewarding.

CONCLUSION

As this book draws to a close, let's promise to ourselves to continue the journey with the same courage and curiosity that started it. Let's commit to being lifelong learners, resilient warriors, deep connectors, and generous mentors. The road ahead is rich with potential, and every step forward is an opportunity to live more fully, love more deeply, and lead more courageously. In the next chapter, we'll reflect on the journey, summarizing the key insights and preparing for a future where these principles become integral to every aspect of our lives. Let's move forward with hope and determination, ready to face whatever challenges and triumphs lie ahead.

FOURTEEN

REFLECTIONS AND RESOLUTIONS – EMBODYING CHANGE FOR A LIFETIME

What you get by achieving your goals is not as important as what you become by achieving your goals.
— Henry David Thoreau

In this final chapter, we reflect on our journey together, distilling the essence of what we've learned and setting resolutions to carry these transformations into the future. This is a time for celebration, gratitude, and contemplation of the road ahead.

REFLECTING ON THE JOURNEY

Let's take a moment to reflect on where we started and where we are now. We began as individuals seeking change—perhaps feeling stuck, unfulfilled, or disconnected. We've considered how to transform our approach to life's challenges and relationships by exploring Unconditional High Regard, Ownership, Self-Reliance, and Brotherhood. We've learned to value ourselves and others more deeply, take responsibility for our happiness, rely on our inner strength, and cherish the support of our community.

CELEBRATING GROWTH

It's important to celebrate the growth we've achieved. Acknowledging our progress helps solidify these changes and reinforces our commitment to this new way of living. Celebrate the significant milestones and the small, everyday victories that have contributed to your transformation. Remember, each step forward, no matter how small, is a part of profound change.

GRATITUDE FOR THE PATH

Gratitude is a powerful tool for maintaining a positive outlook and fostering continued growth. Reflect on the people, experiences, and lessons that have been part of your transformation. Expressing gratitude for these can enhance your appreciation for life and deepen your commitment to your journey.

SETTING FORTH RESOLUTIONS

As we look to the future, let's set resolutions that reflect our continued commitment to these principles. These resolutions might involve:

- Continue to practice daily acts of unconditional high regard.
- Regularly assessing our lives for areas where we can better take ownership.

- Challenging ourselves to rely on our inner strength in new and demanding situations.
- Seeking out or strengthening our Brotherhood, ensuring we have the support and connection we need.

PLANNING FOR CHALLENGES

Change is not without its challenges. Anticipate future obstacles and plan how to apply the keys to overcome them. Consider scenarios that test your commitment to these principles and think through strategies to navigate these challenges while staying true to your growth.

PASSING ON THE LEGACY

Think about how you can pass on what you've learned. You can influence others positively through mentoring, sharing your story, or simply living out these principles visibly and authentically. Your journey could inspire and empower someone else to embark on their own.

CONCLUSION: A LIFETIME OF TRANSFORMATION

As we close this book, remember that this is not the end but the beginning. The journey of personal transformation is a lifetime pursuit. The principles and experiences we've discussed are tools that will continue to serve you well. Keep them close and revisit them often.

Let's step forward with a renewed sense of purpose, equipped with the knowledge that we have the tools to face whatever life throws our way. Commit to living these principles each day, enriching your life and those around you. Let's embrace a future where we continue to grow, love, and lead with courage and compassion.

Here's to a lifetime of learning, growth, and profound transformation!

PART FOUR
WHAT TO DO NEXT

Well done is better than well said.
— Benjamin Franklin

FIFTEEN

JOIN OR CREATE A MEN'S COMMUNITY

Never doubt that a small group of thoughtful, committed citizens can change the world; indeed, it's the only thing that ever has.

— Margaret Mead

CREATING WHAT I NEED MOST

We are not meant to walk alone in our life journey, particularly through its challenging curves. After struggling to find encouragement for my journey for so long, I swore that if I made it through alive, I'd do something about that. I never wanted a man to feel the level of pain, isolation, and confusion I encountered for nearly two decades, seven of which were excruciating. I made it through and fulfilled my oath by creating a community called Masterful Men.

As the founder and principal mentor at Masterful Men, I am proud that my fellow mentors and I have transformed our painful experiences into meaning and purpose that create good in the world. We spend our days offering empathy, compassion, understanding, encouragement, and guidance to men facing profound struggles when dealing with deep-rooted emotional pain, marital frustrations, and the quest for personal fulfillment.

WHY JOIN A BROTHERHOOD?

- Support: Immerse yourself in a brotherhood that offers more than just advice—a community that listens, understands, and stands by you as you navigate your toughest challenges.
- Growth: Benefit from Sven's direct mentorship, drawing from his deep understanding of the emotional and relational issues men face today, helping you unravel the root causes of your struggles.
- Accountability: Forge strong bonds with like-minded men who encourage and challenge you, fostering a space where each member grows together.

Masterful Men is not your average men's group where a bunch of angry, insecure men rally around griping and complaining about how unlucky they are and how bad the women of the world are today. Instead, it's a global movement dedicated to guiding men through experiences of Renewal, Connection, Inspiration, and Empowerment.

Whether you're contemplating the end of a marriage, battling against a tide of resentment, or simply seeking a deeper connection in your relationships, The Masterful Men community offers a beacon of hope and a path to healing.

∼

JOIN ME AT MASTERFUL MEN

JOIN ME AT MASTERFUL MEN AND BEGIN TRANSFORMING YOUR narrative from pain to purpose, frustration to fulfillment. Visit https://become.masterful.men to join a global, private men's community focused on healing from within. Under the guidance of experienced mentors, you can engage in deep, personalized one-on-one or small group sessions. Start your journey of empowerment today—don't let another day pass in isolation. Connect with us to live fully, love deeply, and lead courageously.

Scan the QR Code below with your phone to learn more:

CREATING YOUR OWN BROTHERHOOD

While joining an established community like Masterful Men can provide immense benefits, you may also find that creating your own men's group locally can be equally fulfilling. Starting a brotherhood in your neighborhood or city allows you to tailor the experience and focus on specific needs and interests that resonate most with you and potential members in your area.

WHY START YOUR OWN MEN'S GROUP?

Localization: A local group ensures that all activities and meetings are conveniently accessible, increasing regular participation and engagement.

Customization: You have the freedom to set the agenda, topics, and activities that specifically address the interests and challenges you and your group members face.

Leadership: Initiating a group provides a unique opportunity to develop leadership skills and directly impact your community.

STEPS TO CREATE A MEN'S COMMUNITY:

Creating a men's group needn't be complicated. Here are some simple steps to get you started.

1. **Identify Interest:** Gauge interest in your area by talking to friends, acquaintances or through social media.
2. **Set a Vision:** Define what you want your group to achieve, whether it's personal growth, support during tough times, or discussing topics like marriage, fatherhood, or career challenges.

3. **Organize Meetings:** Start by organizing regular meetings, whether virtual or in-person. These can be informal, and the purpose is to get to know each other and discuss everyone's expectations.
4. **Establish Guidelines:** It's crucial to establish ground rules that all members agree on to foster a safe and supportive environment.
5. **Grow Organically:** Allow the group to grow organically through word of mouth and community involvement. Keep the group's purpose and integrity as you expand.

Creating your own men's community is not just about finding support; it's about building a legacy of brotherhood and positive impact that can transform lives. If you resonate with this vision, I encourage you to take the leap and start a community where your leadership can guide others toward growth and fulfillment.

CONNECT AND EMPOWER:

Remember, the essence of any brotherhood, whether through Masterful Men or your creative initiative, is to create a space where men can openly share, learn, and grow together. Each step you take in building this community brings you closer to transforming your life and that of others around you. Let's forge paths that lead to more robust, more connected lives.

SIXTEEN

STAY CONNECTED AND CONTINUE YOUR JOURNEY

The only impossible journey is the one you never begin.
— Tony Robbins

∿

If you found this book's message helpful for your journey, I invite you to stay connected. Let's continue our relationship and see what unfolds. Here are a few ways to stay connected with me and learn more.

SUBSCRIBE TO MY EMAIL NEWSLETTER

Stay informed and inspired with regular updates sent directly to your inbox. My email newsletter provides insights, success stories, and exclusive content to help you continue your personal and relational growth journey. Subscribe today to ensure you never miss out on new resources and events. Sign up now at www.svenmasterson.com.

REQUEST A COMPLIMENTARY SESSION

I spend the bulk of my time speaking to men and experiencing the kinds of things I share in this book. They're always dumbfounded that my invitation to converse with them is legitimate. Many report that these sessions are among the most profound and honest conversations they've ever experienced. I'd love for you to experience the transformative power of personal mentoring by scheduling a complimentary session with me or one of my fellow mentors in the Masterful Men community. This one-on-one opportunity is excellent for starting your path to deeper connection and personal empowerment. If you want to explore the benefits of mentoring and how it can be tailored to your specific needs, this is a great way to begin.

Request your session at https://svenmasterson.com/free-session

EXPLORE MY WEBSITE(S) FOR THE LATEST

- Resentment To Reconnection:
  https://resentmenttoreconnection.com
- My Personal Site: https://svenmasterson.com
- Masterful Men: https://become.masterful.men

FOLLOW ME ON SOCIAL MEDIA

Join our vibrant community online, where you can engage with other men on similar journeys. Following me on social media lets you stay connected, gain daily inspiration, and participate in a supportive community.

You can find me on several websites, Facebook, YouTube, and Instagram, to share your experiences and learn from others.

SOCIAL MEDIA:

- YouTube: https://www.youtube.com/@SvenMasterson
- Facebook: https://www.facebook.com/MentorSven
- Instagram: https://www.instagram.com/MentorSven

YOUR PATH TO A MORE FULFILLING LIFE AWAITS

Don't navigate your journey alone. Join our community, any community where men will build you up. Engage with valuable content, and take advantage of personalized support tailored to your life's challenges and goals. Together, we can achieve a life of fulfillment, connection, and empowerment.

PART FIVE
YEAH, BUT... (FAQS)

Every man takes the limits of his own field of vision for the limits of the world.
– Arthur Schopenhauer

COMMON QUESTIONS - THE "YEAH BUTS."

It's not uncommon for men to have many questions about these four keys. These concepts and principles take men some time to learn. Below, I've included some of the most common questions I encounter among men. I encourage you to contact me with any questions you don't find addressed below. You can do that by visiting https://resentmenttoreconnec tion.com.

Here are a few of the common questions I hear.

SEVENTEEN

YEAH, BUT...

IF WE ARE SUPPOSED TO BE EMOTIONALLY SELF-RELIANT AND SELF-SOURCE OUR EMOTIONAL NEEDS, WHAT IS THE POINT OF RELATIONSHIPS?

This is one of the most common responses to this message, showing how badly we misunderstand relationships. Unfortunately, many people conflate support—helping another with temporal needs for which they are typically responsible—with dependence—taking on the responsibility for another person's needs.

We've been sold the idea that relationships are places to "get stuff" from one another and that these dependency-based transactions are "love." To be clear, every partnership is fundamentally transactional on some level and includes mutual, reciprocal exchange, and that's okay! Without that, we don't have a relationship but empty and meaningless associations.

The problem isn't what we transact in relationships, but that, because our relationships are not built upon solid foundations of Unconditional High Regard for ourselves and one another, we begin turning into currency these things we can't get from one another, such as our sense of value, worth, significance, esteem, confidence, meaning, purpose, respect, appreciation, benevolence, and several other intangible, often existential needs.

I believe that the point of relationships is to create environments where we share with and support one another along our respective journeys. They're not places to meet mutual, dependency-based neediness but to share mutual, wholeness-based abundance.

86

EIGHTEEN
YEAH, BUT...

WHAT IF MY PARTNER DOESN'T NOTICE
OR APPRECIATE MY EFFORTS TO
CHANGE?

Most men ask this question before they're even willing to think about beginning, and it's a great indication that a man has not yet realized that the reward for making these changes isn't to win external praise and validation from others. The reward of implementing these keys is to be free of that very need. It would be best if you began your transformation journey without trying to guarantee outcomes, or you'll never go on the trip. No one on planet Earth is certain about the future. We all must choose our path without knowing if we'll be successful. Though unlikely, your partner may not notice your changes or be unwilling to let go of their hurt, pain, and suffering. Which offers you the best chances of excellent outcomes - doing nothing or becoming your best?

NINETEEN
YEAH, BUT...

IF I SHOW HER UNCONDITIONAL HIGH REGARD, WON'T SHE JUST WALK ALL OVER ME?

This is a widespread objection to UHR. To be blunt, most men who ask this have pretty poor personal boundaries. They often think they have great personal "boundaries" but mistake their rules for others as "boundaries." They are not the same thing. A boundary represents the limit at which I can no longer continue on a course of action or behavior without disowning some part of myself and my value system, eroding my integrity, and becoming inauthentic.

People don't walk all over others to show them unconditional regard; they walk all over someone who tries to show unconditional *partnership*. Making our regard unconditional should not make our partnership conditional. We must still have stellar boundaries. In my experience mentoring men, men lack solid personal boundaries because they lack UHR for themselves and thus compromise on their integrity for expediency —usually because they fear how being authentic will land with their partner. Behind every man with poor boundaries is a fearful man who doesn't truly realize his value, worth, and significance.

TWENTY
YEAH, BUT...

YOU DON'T UNDERSTAND... MY WIFE [IS A NARCISSIST, WAS ABUSED AS A CHILD, HAS ADHD, SAYS SHE _______, ETC.] - (EVEN HER FAMILY ACKNOWLEDGES IT)!

I do understand, brother. I speak with hundreds of men a year who, like you, are experiencing the grating frustration of navigating their relationship turmoil. 99% of them share similar stories—what I've come to call their "Story of Dysfunction." These are the stories a man crafts to understand why his partner is not like he believes she should be. Let me let you in on a secret... we're all dysfunctional! I guarantee you, your partner, has or has had similar stories, one she uses to understand why you're not the man she imagined you'd be. She's probably shared with her girlfriends, parents, and therapist her theories about why you're not showing up in the relationship as the "ideal man" she wishes you were.

First, you need to know that we all suffer hurtful and painful things in our journeys to one degree or another. Each uniquely shapes and molds us into who we are, how we behave, and how we understand relationships. You and your partner are no different. As the old saying goes, don't wait to find the perfect partner; become one.

The second thing I encourage you to consider is that we all have a part of us (our ego) that has carried around a mental image, often since childhood, of what an ideal mate looks like. Because I am a man, my conception of a perfect woman is quite different than what an *actual* woman is really like. Instead, most men conceive this imaginary woman as a soft, tender man with boobs. She's a woman who is easy to be around, never squawks, is never moody, instantly aroused at the mere thought of sex, and ready for it at all times.

Likewise, your partner has spent a lifetime daydreaming about what an ideal man is like, and to her, that's basically a strong, hairy woman. He's a man who provides endless strength and is perfectly ready to offer endless emotional support, intuitive understanding, and immediate focus and attention. He can do all this and still beat up the bad guys—the perfect combination of Fred Rogers and Chuck Norris.

These conceptions are not reality, yet we immediately begin judging our real-life partner by these standards and feeling disappointed. But, hey… we don't know what I don't know! For long-term relationships to flourish and reach acceptance, we must let these conceptions go and get to know our real-life, flesh-and-blood partner, deciding if we are willing to accept that person as they are, not as we wish they would be.

TWENTY-ONE

YEAH, BUT...

HOW CAN I MAINTAIN UNCONDITIONAL HIGH REGARD WHEN I'M GENUINELY UPSET OR HURT BY SOMEONE'S ACTIONS?

Unconditional High Regard ("UHR") is not sourced in how we emotionally feel about circumstances, including how others think or behave. When we source the decisions of who we will be and how we will act in the ways others are being, we don't own ourselves; others do. Unconditional High Regard is different—it's self-reliant, self-sourced regard we own (Ownership!). It is rooted in making deliberate, decisive decisions despite our emotions.

That doesn't mean we cannot or should not address our deep hurt. We must! Part of our journey (and a massive part of what we do in the Masterful Men community) involves learning about our pain and how to effectively transform it from being our most significant barrier to change to our most enormous opportunity for connection. I recommend you request a complimentary session with a mentor at Masterful Men to learn more about this.

TWENTY-TWO

YEAH, BUT...

WHAT IF I TRY TO TAKE OWNERSHIP, AND IT JUST LEADS TO MORE BLAME FROM OTHERS?

Nearly eight billion people are on the planet during this writing. Many will disagree, misunderstand, think poorly of, and blame you. Hurt people hurt people. Ownership is a powerful force in a man's life and worth living with whether or not others do likewise. Our members routinely express how people who have habitually blamed them begin releasing them from blame as they encounter him doing so. No one likes to be blamed, so when a man starts to release blame for others, the space that used to be filled with blame becomes filled with acceptance for others. Acceptance is the absence of blame. Don't underestimate the transformative power of acceptance.

TWENTY-THREE
YEAH, BUT...

WHAT IF I DON'T HAVE A SUPPORTIVE
BROTHERHOOD OR COMMUNITY TO
TURN TO?

Most men we meet struggle with this, and they nearly all report feelings of isolation. Supportive brotherhood begins when one man has the courage and boldness, to tell the truth about himself to just one other man. If you have the strength to start a supportive brotherhood, create one! If you need encouragement and healing, consider joining the Masterful Men community.

TWENTY-FOUR
YEAH, BUT...

HOW CAN SELF-RELIANCE HELP ME WHEN I FEEL COMPLETELY OVERWHELMED AND UNABLE TO COPE?

Men often feel overwhelmed when they don't know what to do, feel they have no choices and have reached the limit of their trust in themselves to lead forward. This is a common experience; every man will face this eventually. Our natural response, especially when isolated, is to become distraught over our lack of choices. When a man is part of a supportive community, his brothers can help him see new paths, options, and choices.

If you find yourself so overwhelmed that you're experiencing thoughts of self-harm, violence, or suicide, it is crucial to seek immediate help from professionals. Here are some resources available to you:

- National Suicide Prevention Lifeline (U.S.): Call 1-800-273-TALK (1-800-273-8255) for 24/7 free and confidential support for people in distress.
- Crisis Text Line (U.S.): Text HOME to 741741 to connect with a Crisis Counselor.
- International Resources: Please refer to your local health services or visit the International Association

for Suicide Prevention at www.iasp.info for a
directory of resources and contacts in your country.

Remember, reaching out for help is a sign of strength and the first step towards recovery.

TWENTY-FIVE
YEAH, BUT...

WHAT IF MY CIRCUMSTANCES ARE MUCH MORE CHALLENGING THAN YOU'VE DESCRIBED?

I understand that each man's journey is unique, with challenges that may seem impossible from his current vantage point. The principles shared in this book—Unconditional High Regard, Ownership, Self-Reliance, and Brotherhood—have profoundly impacted my life and the lives of many men I've had the privilege to mentor. These keys are designed to be flexible and adaptable, offering a framework tailored to meet various personal circumstances and struggles.

However, it's essential to recognize that while these principles are powerful, they are not a one-size-fits-all solution. I cannot claim that they will work universally for every individual. The effectiveness of these approaches can vary based on many factors, including the complexity of your issues, your current mental and emotional state, and the support systems you have in place.

If you find that your circumstances are particularly severe or complex—perhaps involving deep-seated trauma, mental health issues, or other significant challenges—it may be beneficial to seek professional help in conjunction with applying the insights from this book. Professional therapists or counselors can provide specialized support and treatments tailored to your needs.

This book is intended to guide and inspire you to explore new perspectives and approaches to your challenges. It encourages you to experiment with these principles and adapt them to fit your life. Remember, the journey of transformation is deeply personal, and sometimes, the path may require additional resources beyond what any one book or method can provide.

TWENTY-SIX

YEAH, BUT...

HOW LONG WILL IT TAKE TO SEE REAL CHANGES? I'VE TRIED THINGS BEFORE AND HAVE NOT SEEN ANY LASTING IMPACT.

In my years as a professional men's coach and mentor, I've seen some wild claims about turning around your entire life in as little as seven days. After mentoring hundreds of men through transformation processes, I tell men to expect this process to take 18-24 months. Now, that usually scares most men because they think I'm saying that they'll be experiencing their current level of pain and suffering for a long time.

In reality, real change is only a moment away. Our problem is not creating "real" changes but making them sustainable and lasting and integrating them into our new normal. The scientific literature I've encountered about this concept of neuroplasticity varies. In our community, the 18+ months number is a good average. We also find that the depth and lasting impact of changes a man experiences are generally proportional to how well he consistently stops focusing on people and circumstances outside himself.

TWENTY-SEVEN

YEAH, BUT...

WHAT IF I OPEN UP ABOUT MY VULNERABILITIES, AND IT'S USED AGAINST ME?

Worrying about being vulnerable and then having it turned against you is a valid concern. Many men share this fear—it's both common and deeply personal. Opening up about your vulnerabilities requires a lot of courage, especially in environments that might not seem safe or supportive initially.

The key here is to select who you open up to with care. It's essential to ensure that the people you share your innermost thoughts with are trustworthy and supportive. This might mean gradually sharing and testing the waters with minor disclosures to gauge how they are received before sharing more significant aspects of your struggles.

Moreover, opening up is fundamentally about building trust in others and yourself. It's about creating a foundation where you can be authentic, and your openness leads to deeper connections and mutual support. In my experience and our work at Masterful Men, we emphasize the importance of a supportive community or a brotherhood where vulnerabilities can be shared without fear of judgment or betrayal. A supportive brotherhood is a great place to practice vulnerability in a much lower-stakes environment than a long-term relationship.

Suppose you find yourself in a situation where your openness is used against you. In that case, it may indicate that the environment or the relationship isn't conducive to your growth and well-being. It's a harsh realization but also a vital step in learning to set boundaries and choosing healthier spaces and relationships supporting your healing and growth journey.

Remember, being vulnerable doesn't mean you have to share everything with everyone—it means choosing to be open in ways that foster your growth and connect you with others who respect and support your journey.

TWENTY-EIGHT

YEAH, BUT...

ISN'T FOCUSING SO MUCH ON SELF-IMPROVEMENT JUST ANOTHER FORM OF SELFISHNESS?

That's a thoughtful question, and it's understandable to wonder if focusing on self-improvement could be seen as selfish. The truth is there's a significant difference between self-centeredness and self-improvement. Self-centeredness separates us from others, focusing solely on our needs and desires, often at the expense of those around us. In contrast, self-improvement, especially the kind we advocate for in this book, is about growing in ways that enhance our lives and those around us.

When we work on ourselves and cultivate qualities like Unconditional High Regard, Ownership, Self-Reliance, and Brotherhood, we're not doing it to benefit ourselves. We're doing it to become more capable of contributing positively to our relationships and our communities. It's about expanding our ability to be compassionate, to support others, and to lead in ways that enrich the lives of others.

Think of it this way: if you're on an airplane, you must wear your oxygen mask before helping others. It's not because you value your life more than others but because you can't help anyone if you cannot breathe. Similarly, by improving yourself, you're better equipped to be a supportive partner, a caring father, a dependable friend, and a positive force in your community.

Self-improvement isn't about becoming self-absorbed; it's about becoming the best version of yourself to give your best to the world. It's a balance where focusing on self enables a greater capacity to serve and connect with others.

TWENTY-NINE

YEAH, BUT...

WHAT IF I DON'T HAVE THE RESOURCES OR TIME TO INVEST IN THIS KIND OF PERSONAL GROWTH?

That's a valid concern, and it's essential to recognize that not everyone has the same starting point regarding resources or time. However, I believe in the principle of being faithful to what you do have and making the most out of every opportunity, no matter how small it may seem.

The journey of personal growth is about stretching beyond your limits and challenging your self-limiting beliefs. It's about stepping out of your comfort zone to initiate change, even in small ways. You might feel you lack time or resources, but sometimes, it's about reallocating your resources more effectively. Start small—perhaps with just a few minutes each day focused on a single principle discussed in this book, or engage in short, reflective practices that encourage mindfulness and intentional living.

At Masterful Men, we also understand these challenges and offer various free introductory courses that provide a starting point without financial commitment. These resources are crafted to be accessible and manageable, even for those with tight schedules or limited means. To learn more about our free courses, visit https://svenmasterson.com/courses

Most importantly, engaging with a community like

Masterful Men can significantly amplify your resources through the ROI of brotherhood. Being part of a supportive community often provides expanded perspectives and practical insights that can open doors to new opportunities and resources you might not have been aware of. Brotherhood isn't just about emotional support; it's about pooling collective wisdom and resources, making it easier for each member to grow and succeed.

Investing in personal growth, primarily through community, doesn't just consume resources—it builds them. By committing whatever time and resources you currently have, you will likely find that your capacity to handle more grows along with your personal development.

ACKNOWLEDGMENTS

First and foremost, I am grateful to Abba (No, not 7o's Swedish pop group), in whom I live, move, and have my being. I am grateful for your perfect, undying, and unconditional high regard, for believing the best about me, even when I lose sight of who I am, for giving me freedom from guilt and shame, and for empowering me to own and lead myself, and for answering my plea for good brothers to walk the road with. And to Yeshua, the Alpha, and Omega, in whom all things exist and are held together - the best big brother a human can have.

I am deeply grateful to everyone who contributed to the creation of this book. Many incredible individuals have supported me in my writing, transformation, and growth journey.

My family, especially my wife Zelda and our children, have shown immense patience and encouragement as I've taken the "slow meandering route" to learning the things mentioned in this book. Their love and understanding have been my anchor and joy throughout my tumultuous journey and continue to be a source of joy, strength, and encouragement as I march onward.

Without Zelda's willingness to keep trying, no matter how frustrating things became, this book would not exist, nor would the growth and transformation I've experienced within myself.

I am also profoundly grateful for my parents, who, despite coming from familial challenges and circumstances, still instilled within me and my siblings a love for seeking the truth, compassion, curiosity, and perseverance. Thank you, Dad, for modeling many of these UHR concepts to me as you conducted your affairs in life. Thanks for always encouraging me to do the right thing, even when it's uncomfortable. Thank you, Mom, for a lifetime of challenging and teaching me to think profoundly and never take the easy way out.

I am indebted to my mentors, Ed Gibbons ("Uncle Ed") along with Steve Horsmon and Dan Dore of GoodGuys2Great (https://goodguys2greatmen.com) men, both of whose guidance have been invaluable, and to my fellow brothers at Masterful Men, especially my fellow leaders, Jeff F., Craig V., Brian K., and Andrew G. Thank you for caring for men alongside us and furthering our reach.

To my early readers and the broader community at Masterful Men, your feedback was crucial and transformative in refining this work. Your stories and experiences have not only enriched this journey but are also the heart and soul of this book.

I want to give special thanks to Robert Schneps, without whose persistent prodding to write a book and inspiration this would not have been possible.

Finally, a heartfelt thank you to everyone who believed in this project. This book is not just about my journey but also about our collective spirit and support, which made it possible. It is a testament to our shared commitment to growth and learning.

Let's continue to grow and learn together.

SPECIAL THANKS

Special Thanks

An extra special thanks to my VIP "Trailblazers of Transformation": David Dalton, Craig Vickers, Jay Mitchell, and Jeff Friedman. These men have and continue to offer the entire Masterful Men community and me their generous, enthusiastic, and kind-hearted support and encouragement in our work. Together, we are making a difference, and I am humbled by your participation and thankful for your partnership.

ABOUT SVEN MASTERSON

Sven Masterson is an author, men's coach, mentor, and the founder of Masterful Men, a global community dedicated to helping men break free from cycles of resentment, disconnection, and frustration in their most intimate relationships. Specializing in guiding men through renewal, connection, and empowerment, Sven is passionate about helping men transform conflict into deeper intimacy and trust.

With over 30 years of marriage, parenting, and entrepreneurial experience, Sven understands firsthand the challenges men face when grappling with anger, low intimacy, and feelings of failure in their relationships. Through his work, he offers actionable steps to help men rebuild confidence, emotional resilience, and authentic connection—not just with their partners but with themselves.

Sven's coaching draws on his personal experiences, making his guidance relatable and grounded. He provides a safe and supportive space for men to navigate the emotional pain and self-doubt that often accompany marital struggles, empowering them to take ownership of their growth and lead their relationships with compassion and integrity.

In addition to one-on-one coaching and group sessions, Sven shares his insights through his writing and the Masterful Men community, creating resources that help men untangle their struggles, reclaim their confidence, and reestablish meaningful partnerships. His warm, honest, and down-to-earth approach inspires men to move beyond blame and fear, enabling them to show up as the best version of themselves in their relationships.

Outside of his work, Sven enjoys a simple and intentional life on a rural homestead in North Central Pennsylvania with his wife of 30 years, Zelda, and three of their six children. Together, they embrace the joys of rural living, including gardening, homesteading, and exploring the great outdoors. Sven's journey is a testament to the possibilities that emerge when men take responsibility for their growth and commit to building thriving, connected lives.

facebook.com/MentorSven

x.com/masterfulmen

instagram.com/masterful.men

linkedin.com/in/svenmasterson

amazon.com/stores/Sven-Masterson/author/B0D3YFWY5P

youtube.com/@SvenMasterson

ALSO BY SVEN MASTERSON

NARCISSIST! OR NOT?: A MAN'S GUIDE TO TRANSFORMING HURTFUL ACCUSATIONS INTO LASTING LOVE & TRUST

Have you been called a narcissist? This book challenges harmful labels and provides tools to break free from cycles of defensiveness and conflict. Discover how to cultivate emotional strength, rebuild trust, and create deeper connection in your relationships.

More Info at www.narcissistornot.com

WHAT TO DO WHEN THE ALIENS SHOW UP (AND EVEN IF THEY DON'T): A PRACTICAL GUIDE TO OVERCOMING FEAR, NAVIGATING UNCERTAINTY, AND THRIVING IN ANY CRISIS

Feeling overwhelmed by today's chaotic world? Whether you're facing personal struggles, societal upheaval, or even the possibility of extraterrestrial visitors, this book equips you with the tools to overcome fear, resist manipulation, and thrive in any crisis. Learn how to reclaim your personal power, build resilience, and navigate uncertainty with confidence and clarity.

More Info at www.alienarrivalbook.com

A NOTE TO READERS

Dear Reader,

Thank you for joining me on this journey from resentment to reconnection. Your willingness to explore these challenging emotions and work toward reconnection means a great deal to me.

If this book has touched you in any way, I would be deeply grateful if you would take a moment to share your thoughts in a review where you purchased the book. Your honest feedback helps other readers make informed decisions and contributes to important conversations about healing.

I'd love to hear about your experience with this book. Whether it sparked positive changes in your life or raised concerns you'd like to discuss, please feel free to reach out to me at sven@svenmasterson.com. I am committed to supporting my readers' reconnection journeys and value your perspective.

Thank you for being part of this community of healing.

Warmly,
Sven Masterson

www.ingramcontent.com/pod-product-compliance
Lightning Source LLC
Chambersburg PA
CBHW071329140726

47996CB00005B/1887